Original title:
Night Whispers, Starry Tales

Copyright © 2024 Creative Arts Management OÜ
All rights reserved.

Author: Micah Sterling
ISBN HARDBACK: 978-9916-90-698-9
ISBN PAPERBACK: 978-9916-90-699-6

Journey Through the Ethereal Night

Underneath the silver glow,
Stars whisper secrets to the sea.
The moonlight dances soft and slow,
Guiding dreams where hearts roam free.

Each step unfolds a tale untold,
In shadows deep, where spirits glide.
The night enfolds, a cloak of gold,
Every breath a thrilling ride.

Winds carry scents of blooming grace,
While whispers curl through ancient trees.
The universe's warm embrace,
Wraps us in its mysteries.

With every heartbeat, time suspends,
A symphony of stars aligns.
In this stillness, magic blends,
Eternal peace in black designs.

The Silence that Dances in Dusk

The shadows stretch as day departs,
Whispers of twilight fill our hearts.
Colors blend in soft embrace,
Night arrives with gentle grace.

Crickets sing a lullaby,
Underneath the fading sky.
Stars awaken, shimmering bright,
Guiding us into the night.

Nocturnal Whispers from Ethereal Realms

A breeze carries secrets untold,
In the dark, mysteries unfold.
Moonbeams dance on silver streams,
Weaving tales of silent dreams.

Echoes of laughter float through air,
Stories of wonder linger there.
Glimmers of hope, the night reveals,
Touching the heart with tender feels.

Twilight's Secrets in Velvet Hues

Velvet skies hold secrets deep,
In twilight's arms, the world will leap.
Hues of amber, crimson, and blue,
Painting moments forever true.

A canvas of dreams, fading light,
Capturing whispers of the night.
Each star a spark, a fading thought,
Twilight's lore intricately wrought.

Adventures in the Realm of the Night

In shadows deep, excitement stirs,
Adventures call as the darkness blurs.
Footsteps soft on a moonlit path,
Embracing the night's gentle wrath.

Beneath the stars, we chase the thrill,
Hearts aglow with an ardent will.
Magic weaves through every sigh,
In the realm where dreams never die.

Nocturnal Dreams

In the quietest hour of night,
Whispers dance in silver light.
Stars twinkle like distant eyes,
Cradling secrets, soft and wise.

Shadows waltz upon the floor,
Echoes linger, asking more.
Fleeting visions fade away,
In the twilight where dreams play.

Floating gently on moonbeams,
Lost within our midnight dreams.
Stars align, futures in sight,
Guided by the inner light.

Embrace the stillness, take a breath,
In these moments, feel the depth.
Nocturnal dreams entwine the heart,
Crafting tales where all can start.

Echoes of the Dark

Silence whispers, soft and low,
Through the shadows, secrets flow.
Nighttime breathes, a gentle sigh,
Where the darker spirits lie.

Echoes sound, a haunting call,
In the night, we hear it all.
Memories weave and intertwine,
Lost within the endless line.

Footsteps linger on the ground,
In the stillness, hope is found.
Chasing phantoms, restless flight,
Guided by the faintest light.

In the dark, we face our fears,
Through the silence, shed our tears.
Echoes of the dark align,
In the night, our souls combine.

Moonlit Reveries

Underneath the glowing moon,
Whispers float, a gentle tune.
Golden beams on velvet skin,
Where our wanderings begin.

In the hush, the world stands still,
Hearts awaken, feeling thrill.
Each star holds a wish to share,
Floating dreams beyond compare.

Time suspends in silver light,
Guiding us through endless night.
With each glance, a story spun,
Together 'neath the midnight sun.

Moonlit paths where shadows play,
Love's sweet song will find a way.
In the silence, we can see,
Reveries of what could be.

Cosmic Conversations

Beneath the vast, eternal sky,
Stars converse, and comets fly.
Whispers of the universe,
In its breath, we feel the verse.

Galaxies twirl in endless waltz,
In their dance, we find our pulse.
Time and space a tapestry,
Woven threads of mystery.

Answers hide in cosmic light,
In their glow, we chase the night.
Planets hum a lullaby,
Echoing in the heart's sigh.

In each twinkle, wisdom shared,
Through the echoes, souls prepared.
Cosmic conversations guide,
As we walk this stellar tide.

Soft Chants of the Evening

The sun dips low in gentle glow,
Shadows stretch, they come and go.
Birds sing sweet in twilight's hold,
Nature's tales softly told.

Cool winds brush against the trees,
Carrying whispers, sweet as dreams.
Stars awaken, twinkle bright,
As day surrenders to the night.

Murmurs of the Infinite

In the vastness where silence reigns,
Echoes of thought, breaking chains.
Galaxies dance in cosmic play,
Whispers of time, night and day.

Each star holds a story untold,
A mystery waiting to unfold.
The universe sways in gentle grace,
In the infinite's warm embrace.

Enigmas of Dusk

Dusk weaves shadows, deep and long,
A tapestry, both soft and strong.
Secrets linger in fading light,
As day dissolves into the night.

The sky dons hues of purple and grey,
Where the sun and moon gently play.
Each moment holds a fleeting glance,
An enigma wrapped in evening's dance.

Luminous Whispers

In the stillness, whispers call,
Like starlight's touch, they softly fall.
Moonbeams traverse the quiet ground,
Illuminating the world around.

Secrets shared in shimmering beams,
Echo of forgotten dreams.
Gentle voices, soft and clear,
Luminous whispers, drawing near.

Echoes in the Silence

Whispers dance upon the air,
In shadows deep, secrets lay bare.
Moonlight weaves through night's embrace,
Echoes call from a forgotten place.

Stars reply with soft, sweet sighs,
As stillness wraps the world in ties.
In silence, hearts begin to hear,
The melody of dreams held dear.

Faintest sounds of love and loss,
In twilight's glow, they stitch the cross.
Each echo sends a pulse alive,
A timeless thread where spirits strive.

Listen close, let the night unfold,
In whispers soft, our tales retold.
With every breath, in silence found,
The heart's true song begins to sound.

Enchanted Tranquility

In a garden where the lilies sigh,
Beneath the gaze of the luminous sky.
Every petal a story to weave,
In tranquil moments, we learn to believe.

Rippling waters gently speak,
Of peace found in the still and meek.
A breeze carries secrets from afar,
Whispering dreams where wishes are.

In soft embrace, nature unfolds,
A tapestry rich with colors bold.
The heart finds solace, free from strife,
In enchanted pools of serene life.

Let every breath be a soothing sound,
In this haven where love is found.
Embrace the calm, let worries cease,
In this enchanted world, find your peace.

Phosphorescent Dreams

In the depths where shadows play,
Glows the light of night's ballet.
Flickering hopes in glimmering beams,
Guide the heart through phosphorescent dreams.

Ocean waves dance, their secrets bright,
In luminescence, they share their light.
Whispers of stars upon the sea,
Are the dreams that set us free.

With every twinkle, a story shared,
Of journeys daring and hearts unpaired.
Through the darkness, let visions gleam,
Awakening souls to the world's grand scheme.

Embrace the night, where wonders reside,
In phosphorescent glow, let hope abide.
For in dream's embrace, we learn to soar,
And find our way to a brighter shore.

Lullabies of the Celestial Veil

Beneath the stars, the nightingale calls,
Singing softly as moonlight falls.
Wrapped in warmth of twilight's embrace,
Lullabies weave through time and space.

Cradled in the arms of dreams untold,
With whispers of wishes softly bold.
Each note a wish upon the air,
A symphony of love beyond compare.

Clouds may drift, but hopes remain,
In lullabies, we find the gain.
The universe hums a gentle tune,
Drawing hearts closer beneath the moon.

So close your eyes, let the night unfold,
In celestial dreams, let your heart be bold.
For every star is a promise made,
In lullabies of the infinite shade.

Faint Flickers

In twilight's hush, soft shadows play,
Faint flickers dance, then drift away.
Whispers of light in gentle grace,
A fleeting touch, a warm embrace.

Stars emerge, a twinkling maze,
Guiding hearts through the night's haze.
Each spark a wish, a silent plea,
In dreams we find what's meant to be.

Echoes of laughter, memories glow,
In the stillness, time moves slow.
Faint flickers fade, yet still they stay,
In the heart, forever play.

Starlit Memories

Beneath the sky where wishes soar,
Starlit memories we can't ignore.
Each shimmering dot, a story told,
Of love and laughter, dreams of old.

Time may pass, yet we recall,
Moments that bind us, through it all.
A nostalgic glance, a soft sigh,
Under the stars, we still fly high.

Fleeting glances, a shared delight,
In the shadows of the night.
As constellations softly gleam,
We cherish every whispered dream.

Beyond the Horizon's Edge

Waves crash softly on golden sands,
Beyond the horizon, fate makes its plans.
Where sky meets sea, and dreams collide,
A world awaits on the other side.

Colors merge in the evening flush,
The sun dips low, creating a hush.
Adventures call from the distant shore,
Beyond the horizon, we'll find much more.

With hearts as sails, we journey wide,
Guided by hope, and the rising tide.
In every wave, a new start,
Beyond the horizon, we chart our heart.

Enchanted Veils

In forests deep, where secrets lie,
Enchanted veils of mist float by.
Whispers of magic in the air,
A world of wonders, beyond compare.

Branches sway with a gentle tune,
Under the watch of a silver moon.
Each step we take, the earth replies,
With stories hidden from prying eyes.

Petals fall like a dream's soft sigh,
In twilight's glow, time seems to fly.
Through enchanted veils, we wander free,
In nature's arms, just you and me.

Soft Hits of the Celestial Drum

In the hush of night, a rhythm plays,
Echoes through the velvet, soft and deep.
A heartbeat of the cosmos, gently sways,
Awakening the dreams we long to keep.

Beneath the glowing moon, we find our peace,
In melodies that dance upon the air.
The universe hums, sweet songs release,
Each note a whisper, a gentle prayer.

Stars shimmer bright, responding in time,
Each hit a story, of love and loss.
Harmony entwined, a celestial rhyme,
In the silence, the world's urgent gloss.

So close your eyes, let the music flow,
With every pulse, we learn to embrace.
The soft hits resound, in peaceful glow,
A drumbeat of hope, eternal grace.

Spirit Songs of the Twilight

As dusk embraces, the sky ignites,
A canvas brushed with hues so divine.
In twilight whispers, the spirit ignites,
Echoes of stories, in shadows they twine.

The breeze carries secrets, from ages past,
Soft melodies woven in night's warm quilt.
Each note is a candle, a flame to last,
Illuminate paths where the dreams are built.

Beneath the starlight, soft voices blend,
With laughter and tears from the night's embrace.
The songs of spirits around us extend,
Bridging our hearts in this sacred space.

twilight fades, yet the song remains,
A tapestry woven with love and light.
In spirit's embrace, we break the chains,
Finding our way through the sheltering night.

Celestial Mosaic

Upon the canvas of the stretchéd sky,
Stars scatter like jewels, bright and bold.
Each a story, a wish, a silent why,
Together they form a picture untold.

Nebulae swirl, in colors unchained,
A dance of creation, wild and free.
In cosmic tides where the heartbeat is gained,
Mosaics of beauty, for all eyes to see.

Galaxies spin, in a whirl of dreams,
Entwined in the silence of vastness profound.
Light years apart, yet together it seems,
Each spark a reminder, we're forever bound.

So gaze upon the sky, let your soul soar,
Embrace the wonder, the endless expanse.
In the celestial art, we are evermore,
A mosaic of life in a timeless dance.

Whispers of Wandering Stars

In the quiet night, stars begin to roam,
Each one a traveler, seeking its fate.
Whispers of journeys, where spirits call home,
Infinite stories wrapped in stardust's weight.

They twinkle and glide, like dreams on the brink,
Echoes of ages, they silently trust.
In the vast tapestry, they weave and link,
A dance of memories, of hope and dust.

Each star a guardian, watching from high,
Guiding the wanderers, lost in their quest.
In the stillness, hear their sigh,
A lullaby sweet, a celestial jest.

So follow the light, with eyes open wide,
Embrace the enchantment of night's gentle song.
The whispers of stars, in starlit tide,
Carry us onward, where we all belong.

Celestial Murmurs

Whispers of stars in the night,
Softly they dance, pure delight.
A lullaby floats on the breeze,
Cradled in dreams, hearts at ease.

Galaxies spin in silent grace,
Infinite wonders, a vast embrace.
Constellations weave tales so old,
In the night sky, secrets unfold.

Nebulae glow, a vibrant hue,
Painted skies in a cosmic view.
Echoes of light from ages past,
In the stillness, spells are cast.

Moonbeams trace shadows on the ground,
In their softness, solace is found.
With each twinkle, a story is spun,
In celestial murmurs, we are one.

Twilight Secrets

Beneath the veil of fading light,
Shadows stretch, whispering night.
Secrets linger in the twilight,
Where day and dreams soon take flight.

Colors blend in soft repose,
Petals close as evening shows.
The sky blushes, a gentle sigh,
As the stars begin to rise high.

Echoes of day start to wane,
Nightfall brings a sweet refrain.
Mysteries wrapped in dusky hues,
In twilight's arms, the world renews.

Each breath carries a tale untold,
In the silence, magic unfolds.
With twilight comes a sacred peace,
In dimming light, our worries cease.

Lullabies of the Cosmos

Softly the stars begin to hum,
In the cradle of night, we become.
Lullabies of the cosmos sing,
A soothing balm that the heavens bring.

Planets spin in a gentle waltz,
The universe sways, and our hearts pulse.
With each note, our spirits soar,
In celestial symphonies, we explore.

Stardust floats like whispers bright,
Telling tales of distant light.
Galactic dreams in slumber deep,
In these lullabies, the universe sleeps.

As time unravels, we drift away,
In cosmic arms, we long to stay.
Each lullaby a wish from afar,
Guided by the light of a distant star.

Stellar Serenades

In the deep of night, melodies play,
Stars twinkle softly, guiding the way.
Stellar serenades fill the air,
A cosmic rhythm, beyond compare.

Planets gather in a celestial line,
Their orbits dance, a grand design.
Harmony sings through the void so wide,
With each note, galaxies collide.

Whispers of comets breeze on by,
As meteors streak across the sky.
Celestial choirs in harmony blend,
In stellar nights, where dreams ascend.

Let the universe cradle your soul,
In the music of stars, we are whole.
With every twinkle, a promise made,
In these stellar serenades, we wade.

Serenade of Celestial Shadows

In the hush of night, whispers play,
Soft notes drift on the cool wind's sway.
Stars above twinkle, serene and bright,
Creating a dance in the velvet night.

Moonbeams stretch and gently tease,
Nature hums a tune with ease.
Every shadow holds a dream,
In the serenade, life does gleam.

Beneath the Gaze of Flickering Lights

City streets glow with warmth and grace,
Each corner holds a familiar face.
Laughter echoes, a sweet serenade,
Beneath the stars, memories are made.

Flickering lights tell tales of old,
Adventures whispered, secrets told.
Moments captured in the night's embrace,
Under the watch of time and space.

Mysterious Murmurs from the Dark

In the silence, shadows softly creep,
Murmurs of the night, secrets to keep.
The moon casts a glance, knowing all,
While the night weaves its enigmatic thrall.

Rustling leaves share stories untold,
Ancient echoes of bravery bold.
In the dark, magic swirls like mist,
Leaving the heart longing, never missed.

Tales Woven in Starlight Threads

Starlight dances across the skies,
Tales are woven where dreams arise.
Each twinkle holds a story rare,
A glimpse of wonders beyond compare.

With every heartbeat, legends play,
In whispers of night, they find their way.
Threads of fate, intricate and fine,
Weaving the cosmos, both yours and mine.

When Darkness Tells Its Stories

In whispers low, the shadows creep,
They weave the tales that silence keep.
Each secret shared, a haunting song,
In the quiet night, where dreams belong.

The stars above, like eyes that see,
Bear witness to our history.
An echo of a time long past,
In darkness' grip, the die is cast.

Ghosts of the heart, they softly call,
In twilight's veil, we hear them all.
With every sigh, a memory burns,
As deep within our spirit yearns.

So let us listen to the night,
For in her depths, we find our light.
When darkness speaks, we must believe,
In every story, we learn to grieve.

Illuminated Echoes of Forgotten Realms

Beneath the glow of ancient skies,
Whispers float where the time flies.
Forgotten dreams, like shadows cast,
In glimmers bright, the sail is massed.

Each echo shared in golden beams,
Awakens finally our wild dreams.
The realms we lost, they softly sigh,
In lands where memories never die.

With every light that fades away,
The past ignites in dreams of gray.
Illuminated paths we roam,
To find the echoes, bring us home.

So take my hand, let's softly tread,
Through realms where all the stories spread.
In luminous hues, we shall explore,
The echoes calling forevermore.

Beneath the Luminescent Canopy

Underneath the stars so bright,
We find our peace in the quiet night.
The branches sway, a gentle dance,
As dreams awaken, we take a chance.

With every rustle in the leaves,
A list of hopes that heart believes.
Beneath the glow of silver light,
Our wishes soar in pure delight.

The world above begins to fade,
In nature's arms, our fears betrayed.
The canopy, a soothing balm,
Wraps us in safety, still and calm.

So hush your thoughts, let silence sing,
Beneath the stars, our spirits cling.
In this embrace, our hearts align,
As twilight whispers, forever divine.

The Moon's Soft Embrace of Reminiscence

In silver light, the moon does gleam,
Caressing memories like a dream.
Each flicker tells a tale of yore,
In gentle waves, we long for more.

The night unfolds its velvet cloak,
As whispered thoughts, like shadows, stoke.
In lunar beams, our past is found,
A soft embrace, where hearts are bound.

With every rise and fall of tide,
The moon's reflected tears abide.
In her glow, our stories play,
A dance of hours, come what may.

So let us linger in her gaze,
For time suspended, in her phase.
In the moon's embrace, we reminisce,
Finding solace in the night's pure bliss.

The Dreamer's Guide to Celestial Journeys

In the realm where stardust flows,
Wander the paths where moonlight glows.
Each twinkling star, a tale untold,
Adventures beckon, brave and bold.

Through cosmic winds, the dreamers soar,
Past the comets and planets galore.
Galaxies whisper, inviting the soul,
Embrace the journey, let it unfold.

With nebulae bright as guides in the night,
Dreamers dance with delight in flight.
In the silence of space, they find their tune,
Cradled softly by the silver moon.

So take your heart and let it be free,
On celestial waves, in endless decree.
For in every dream, a star may ignite,
Leading you home through the velvet night.

Whispers of Time in the Universe's Arms

Time flows gently in cosmic streams,
Wrapped in the fabric of endless dreams.
Moments linger like echoes of light,
Carrying tales through the folds of night.

Each tick of the clock, a whisper so sweet,
In the depths of the void where shadows meet.
Stars listen closely to secrets we share,
In the vastness of space, we're beyond compare.

Planets revolve in their timeless dance,
As the universe holds us in a trance.
With every heartbeat, the cosmos sighs,
A gentle reminder of how time flies.

So breathe in the essence, let moments weave,
In the universe's arms, we learn to believe.
For every heartbeat is a story, a chime,
In the infinite circles of space and time.

Tales from a Darkened Sky

Under the veil of a starless night,
Shadows gather, cloaked in fright.
Whispers of winds weave through the dark,
A tapestry of tales waiting to spark.

Lost souls wander in search of a path,
Guided by pain, shadows' quiet wrath.
Moons hide their glow, stars cease to shine,
Yet still, the heart hopes for a sign.

Each gust of wind carries secrets old,
Ancient stories of love, brave and bold.
From the depths of silence, voices arise,
Echoing softly, under darkened skies.

But from this abyss comes a flicker of light,
A promise that dawn will conquer the night.
Though dark might prevail, it will not persist,
For every shadow awaits the sun's kiss.

The Gentle Hand of Midnight

Midnight descends with a soothing embrace,
Wrapping the world in its velvet grace.
Stars twinkle softly, a lullaby sung,
As time pauses gently, forever young.

Whispers of dreams drift in the air,
Calling the wanderers lost in despair.
With each gentle breeze, hope finds its way,
Guiding the weary till the break of day.

In the depths of night, shadows take flight,
Carrying wishes into the height.
The moonlight kisses the earth from above,
Filling the darkness with warmth and love.

So let the midnight cradle your soul,
In its tender arms, feel completely whole.
For when the world sleeps, magic is real,
In the gentle hand of night, we heal.

Veils of the Night

The moonlight glimmers soft and bright,
Casting shadows in the night.
Whispers dance on breezes light,
Stars awaken, taking flight.

In the silence, secrets weave,
Tales of hearts that dare believe.
Mysteries the dark conceives,
With the dawn, they gently leave.

Crickets sing a serenade,
While the dusk begins to fade.
In this world, true dreams are made,
Finding peace in twilight's shade.

Veils that shroud the dreams we seek,
Follow paths both bold and meek.
In the night, our spirits speak,
In the dark, our hearts grow weak.

Woven Dreams

In the fabric of the night,
Dreams are stitched with threads of light.
Each a story, every sight,
Woven with the heart's delight.

Lullabies on gentle waves,
Flow through minds like hidden caves.
In those depths, our spirit braves,
Rising high as courage saves.

Colors swirl in endless dance,
Eager hearts grasp every chance.
In the dream's enchanting glance,
Hope ignites a timeless romance.

Woven threads of fate we find,
Knit together, intertwined.
In the silence, love is kind,
Beyond the veil, our souls aligned.

Chronicles of the Celestial Sphere

In the heavens, stories bloom,
Tales of joy, and hints of gloom.
Stars align in cosmic room,
Where the universe finds its loom.

Each constellation tells a tale,
Of ancient dreams that will not pale.
Guided by the moon's soft veil,
Celestial paths, we set to sail.

Galaxies whisper secrets bright,
In the canvas of the night.
Endless wonders, pure delight,
Chronicles of the endless flight.

Through the cosmos, we will roam,
Finding light, we call it home.
In this vast and starry dome,
Together, we forever comb.

Whims of the Universe

The universe plays its tune,
Dancing stars, a silver rune.
Planets spin and drift in June,
While the sun drapes light like a boon.

In chaos, patterns we can see,
Whispers float on cosmic spree.
Every pulse, a symphony,
Of potential, wild and free.

Galaxies swirl, a playful show,
In infinite space, we freely flow.
With every turn, our spirits grow,
In the whims of time's gentle flow.

Embrace the mystery, take a chance,
In the void, we find our dance.
With the stars, we share a glance,
In the universe's wild romance.

Whispers from the Abyss

In shadows deep, the secrets weave,
Echoes of dreams, where few believe.
A haunting call, from depths below,
Guiding the lost, through ebb and flow.

Eternal night, the silence speaks,
To weary hearts, and fragile peaks.
With every whisper, fear takes flight,
In the abyss, there shines a light.

Voices entwined, like threads of fate,
Unraveling stories, or sealing slate.
What lies beneath, the mind's own test,
In the abyss, are we truly blessed?

From darkness sprung, new paths arise,
A journey shared, where truth defies.
Though shadows lurk, and doubts persist,
The whispers call, we can't resist.

A Dance with the Stars

Under the cloak of velvet skies,
They sway and twirl, where wonder lies.
A cosmic waltz, in rhythms bold,
Stories of love, in stardust told.

Each flicker bright, a heartbeat's trace,
Whispers of dreams, in endless space.
They spin and glide, as night unfolds,
A serenade, that never grows old.

Constellations map the hidden fate,
In spectral hues, they illuminate.
A breath away, from earthly bounds,
In celestial arms, a joy profound.

Together they dance, in timeless grace,
A ballet born from the vast embrace.
Through endless night, their spirits soar,
In the dance of stars, we seek for more.

Ethereal Breaths

In tender hues, the dawn appears,
As whispers drift, like feathered cheers.
The world awakens, fresh and bright,
Each breath a promise, a spark of light.

With every sigh, the spirits rise,
In sacred moments, beneath the skies.
A fluttering pulse, in twilight's glow,
Each ethereal breath, a chance to grow.

Misty veils, where silence dwells,
Cradling secrets, the heart compels.
In the quiet, our hopes take flight,
In ethereal breaths, we find our might.

Embrace the stillness, let it mend,
As tendrils of time begin to blend.
In the dance of life, both soft and bold,
Ethereal breaths, a story told.

Galaxies in the Gloom

In twilight's grip, where shadows play,
Galaxies whisper, in a muted sway.
A tapestry spun, of hope and despair,
In the heart of darkness, we lay bare.

Stars flicker softly, like distant dreams,
Hidden among life's tangled seams.
In the gloom, their light endures,
Guiding the lost, with love that secures.

Nebulas swirl, in colors bold,
Tales of the brave, and those who fold.
In the vast unknown, our fears take flight,
Galaxies spark, igniting the night.

Through the fog, we reach for the grand,
For galaxies in the gloom, we stand.
In every shadow, a glimmer shines,
A cosmic dance, where fate aligns.

Tales of the Orbiting Spheres

In the depths of space they twirl,
Planets dance, a cosmic swirl.
Stars ignite in endless night,
Whispers of the infinite light.

Moons reflect the sun's warm glow,
Silent stories only they know.
Galaxies spin their timeless tale,
Across the void, they gently sail.

Wonders etched in starlit skies,
Guardians of the ancient ties.
Each rotation speaks of fate,
Tales of love, and worlds await.

Orbiting spheres in harmony,
Songs of space, a shared symphony.
With every path, a journey new,
Boundless dreams in the cosmic blue.

Mysteries in the Mist

Veils of fog, secrets unfold,
Whispers hidden, stories told.
Through the shroud, shadows glide,
Ethereal forms, a ghostly ride.

Nature's breath, a mystery spun,
Softly weaving magics won.
Footsteps echo, lost and found,
In this silence, truth is bound.

Through the valley, moonlight streams,
Shattering the realm of dreams.
Every shimmer carries weight,
In the mist, we navigate.

Entwined in twilight, hearts entwine,
With each heartbeat, stars align.
Through the haze, we slowly dance,
Chasing shadows, lost in chance.

Celestial Legends

Ancient myths in twilight's glow,
Cosmic tales from long ago.
Heroes brave on starlit quests,
Their legends spoken, never rest.

In the sky, their story shines,
Constellations draw the lines.
Guiding travelers through the night,
With whispers sweet, a gentle light.

Fates entwined in the astral sea,
Echoes of who we long to be.
As comets blaze, they leave their mark,
In every heart, a fiery spark.

Celestial wonders hold us near,
In every legend, we find cheer.
The cosmos spins its timeless rhyme,
In the tapestry of space and time.

Hushed Hours

In quiet corners, moments blend,
Time slows down, our thoughts extend.
Hushed hours cradle whispered dreams,
Underneath the moon's soft beams.

Shadows linger, softly sway,
Embracing night, as night must stay.
Heartbeats sync with stars above,
In these hours, we find our love.

With every breath, the world stands still,
In the silence, emotions thrill.
Wrapped in arms, we feel the grace,
In hushed hours, we find our place.

As dawn approaches, whispers fade,
Yet in the stillness, memories laid.
Hushed hours linger in our heart,
A tender bond that won't depart.

Ghosts of Dusk

Whispers weave in twilight's lace,
Figures dance with silent grace,
Memories blend with the fading light,
Ghosts of dusk take their flight.

Leaves rustle in a gentle breeze,
Secrets linger among the trees,
The day surrenders, the shadows bloom,
Embracing night, they cloak the gloom.

In the dark, lost voices call,
Echoes rise, then gently fall,
A haunting song, a soft refrain,
Carried forth, yet never vain.

Starlit paths invite the brave,
Through the past, into the grave,
As shadows merge with the soon-to-be,
Ghosts of dusk set the spirit free.

Chasing the Moonbeam

A silver light on rippling seas,
Dancing softly, whispers tease,
Chasing dreams in the night's embrace,
Hopes illuminated, finding grace.

Footsteps follow where shadows play,
Guided by the night's ballet,
Stars shimmer like a distant song,
In the quiet where we belong.

Every sigh, a secret shared,
In the gleam, no heart is scared,
We weave through stories painted bright,
Chasing the moonbeam's silver light.

Though dawn approaches, time runs thin,
Our laughter lingers, we shall win,
Embracing dreams that gently gleam,
Together we'll chase the moonbeam.

Shadows Tell Tales

In the corners where light retreats,
Old shadows dance, their rhythm beats,
Every flicker, a tale untold,
Whispers linger, brave and bold.

Figures linger, stories weave,
In every shadow, we believe,
A tapestry of joy and strife,
Shadows echo the pulse of life.

Beneath the stars, the quiet sigh,
Silent tales that never die,
Flickering forms in the moon's soft glow,
Guardians of secrets only they know.

Take a breath as night unfurls,
In shadows, the world gently whirls,
Listen close, let the night trails,
Every shadow has its tales.

Echoes of the Universe

In the silence, echoes surge,
Whispers from where worlds converge,
Footfalls soft on stardust paths,
Time and space in gentle wraths.

Waves of light in cosmic dance,
Galaxies spin, a timeless chance,
Understanding flows like rivers deep,
Journeys taken, promises to keep.

In the vastness, hearts unfold,
Stories woven, dreams retold,
Each heartbeat echoes, strong and true,
In the universe, we find our view.

Connections spark in night's embrace,
On this journey, we find our place,
With every echo that we find,
Together, we will intertwine.

Secrets Beneath the Sky

Whispers of the night do call,
Stars above watch over all.
Moonlight dances on the ground,
In its glow, the truth is found.

Each shadow hides a tale untold,
In the dark, the brave, the bold.
Secrets linger in the breeze,
Carried softly through the trees.

Glimmers spark the silent dreams,
What is real is not what seems.
In the stillness, hearts will sigh,
Echoes lost beneath the sky.

Underneath the velvet night,
A world waits, hidden from sight.
Step beyond the veil of fear,
Whisper secrets, draw them near.

Fables of the Milky Way

Stars that shimmer, tales are spun,
In the vastness, dreams begun.
Nebulas swirl, colors bright,
Guiding lost souls in the night.

Galaxies dance in endless waltz,
Stories formed in cosmic vaults.
Each star a hope, a wish bestowed,
Fables woven, truth bestowed.

Comets trace their fiery trails,
Whispers echo, ancient tales.
Planets spin with secrets deep,
Guardians of the night, they keep.

Through the ages, myths still grow,
Constellations, legends flow.
In the dark, let spirits play,
Lost within the Milky Way.

Silent Musings

In the quiet, thoughts arise,
Whispers soft as twilight skies.
Gentle breezes stir the mind,
In the silence, peace we find.

Moments linger, time stands still,
Quiet echoes, softly fill.
Words unspoken take their flight,
Painting dreams upon the night.

Reflections dance on tranquil seas,
Rustling leaves, a tender breeze.
In the stillness, voices blend,
Silent musings, heart to mend.

As dawn approaches, light will break,
In the hush, each soul will wake.
Yet still, I cherish what I hear,
In the silence, love is near.

Midnight Stories

Underneath the silver glow,
Time for tales, let shadows grow.
In the hush, the firewood cracks,
Bringing forth the heart's relax.

Stories whispered, voices low,
Ancient legends start to flow.
Fables woven with delight,
Lost in dreams of endless night.

Adventures born in whispered breath,
Voices dance with life and death.
In the dark, our fears take flight,
Yet courage blooms with every fright.

Midnight hours bring solace sweet,
In every tale, our spirits meet.
Gather 'round, forget the past,
In these stories, we are cast.

Celestial Dreams on a Wistful Horizon

Stars whisper secrets in the night,
As the moon casts dreams, soft and bright.
From horizons far, wishes take flight,
In the dance of shadows, hearts unite.

Waves of starlight ripple and flow,
In the quiet of dusk, where wishes grow.
A tapestry woven with threads aglow,
Guiding lost souls through night's gentle show.

On the brink of dawn, where colors swirl,
Each dream awakens, a precious pearl.
In celestial realms, time starts to unfurl,
As we chase the visions, that softly twirl.

With whispers of hope, the cosmos sings,
Of love transcending on silver wings.
In the heart of night, what joy it brings,
Celestial dreams, the universe clings.

Echoes of Hidden Galaxies

In the silence of night, echoes arise,
Hidden galaxies dance in our eyes.
Softly they shimmer, like whispered sighs,
In realms of wonder, curiosity lies.

Each star a story, a life once lived,
Fragments of light to the cosmos give.
Through time and space, they learn to forgive,
In the heart of the dark, the light shall thrive.

Infinite echoes that linger in time,
Carried on whispers, a soft chime.
In constellations, the verses rhyme,
As the universe paints, sublime and prime.

Through telescopes old, we glimpse the past,
In mysteries spun, our shadows cast.
Hidden galaxies, their magic vast,
In the fabric of space, forever to last.

Luminary Tales of Deepest Shadows

In the depths of night, shadows do speak,
Tales of the luminary, bold yet meek.
Each darkness holds secrets, bright streaks,
In the silence of stars, our spirits seek.

Flickers of light in the black, profound,
Guiding our paths, where hope is found.
With every heartbeat, their rhythm's sound,
In the grand tapestry, we're tightly bound.

Shadows dance lightly in the moon's embrace,
Whispers of time, each moment a trace.
In luminary tales, we find our place,
Through the darkest nights, love's gentle grace.

As dawn breaks softly, shadows recede,
Yet the tales remain, a timeless creed.
In every heart, the stories we need,
Illuminating paths, like a faithful steed.

Fantasies Carved in the Night's Canvas

The night spreads its cloak, a canvas vast,
Where fantasies whisper, shadows cast.
With stars as brushes, dreams held fast,
In the quiet corners, silence amassed.

A moonlit story, woven with care,
Imprints of thoughts, floating in air.
In cosmic art, there's magic rare,
Each glimmer a promise, a whispered prayer.

Waves of starlight, in motion they glide,
In the heart of dreams, where wishes bide.
On the canvas of night, our hopes collide,
Creating a world, where spirits reside.

As dawn begins to gently unfurl,
The fantasies fade, in a soft swirl.
Yet in every heart, they will twirl,
Carved in the night, like a precious pearl.

Tales of Celestial Beauty

In the hush of night, stars gleam bright,
Whispers of dreams take fearless flight.
Moonlight dances on silver beams,
Painting the world in shimmering dreams.

Galaxies spin in endless grace,
Echoes of time in boundless space.
Each twinkle tells of ancient lore,
A cosmic tale forevermore.

Comets streak through the velvet sky,
Carving paths where wishes fly.
Nebulas bloom in colors rare,
Nature's canvas beyond compare.

In this vastness, hearts unite,
Embracing magic in the night.
Celestial beauty, a timeless cue,
A reminder of dreams, forever true.

Flickering Echoes

Whispers linger in the twilight,
Flickering echoes, soft and slight.
Shadows dance upon the wall,
Memories whisper, gently call.

Fading laughter in the breeze,
Carried softly through the trees.
Every sound a story shares,
Fragments of life, laid bare.

Chasing hopes on moonlit streams,
Embers glow with fervent dreams.
In this moment, time suspends,
A tapestry that never ends.

Every heartbeat, every sigh,
Threads of life that never die.
Flickering echoes, soft and clear,
A symphony for all to hear.

Diaries of the Stars

Pages turning in the night,
Diaries of stars, filled with light.
Each entry whispers tales untold,
Of love and loss, of brave and bold.

Constellations weave their fate,
Stories twisted, never late.
In every sparkle, history lies,
A tapestry in the skies.

Galactic winds blow through the pages,
Tales of wanderers through the stages.
From stardust born, to dust we return,
Lessons of life, we slowly learn.

Sleepy eyes gaze at the ink,
Moments captured, lost in think.
In their glow, our hearts partake,
Diaries of stars, a wondrous wake.

Unwritten Legends

Legends linger in the air,
Untold stories everywhere.
Echoes of heroes long gone by,
Whispers of truths that never die.

Beneath the moon's soft glowing gaze,
Timeless myths through a smoky haze.
Through ancient woods where shadows play,
Unwritten legends still find a way.

Every heartbeat, a tale to tell,
Of triumphs and trials, all too well.
In the silence, history breathes,
Carving paths where memory weaves.

The future writes upon the past,
Legends alive, connections vast.
In every soul, stories persist,
Unwritten legends, shadows kissed.

Chronicles of Dusk

As daylight fades, the shadows creep,
A world transformed, where silence weeps.
The sky ablaze with hues of gold,
Whispering tales that must be told.

A fleeting moment, dusk's embrace,
Carrying dreams to a hidden place.
Stars awaken, one by one,
A canvas painted, night begun.

In twilight's glow, secrets arise,
Reflections dance in twilight skies.
Echoes of laughter, soft and light,
Embracing all in the velvet night.

The moon ascends, a silver gleam,
Guiding wanderers through the dream.
With every heartbeat, we unite,
In chronicles spun by fading light.

Dreamscapes in the Void

In the void where silence reigns,
A tapestry of dreams remains.
Floating whispers, soft and clear,
In this realm, there's naught to fear.

Stars entwined in a cosmic dance,
Inviting souls to take a chance.
Each heartbeat echoes, a sacred sound,
In dreamscapes lost, yet found.

Time dissolves in twilight haze,
Moments linger, a gentle phase.
Visions shift in luminous streams,
Carving paths through layered dreams.

Awake or slumber, none can tell,
Where the boundaries blur and swell.
In the void, we chase the light,
Lost in dreams of pure delight.

Galactic Whispers

Beneath the stars, a tale untold,
Galactic whispers, brave and bold.
Luminous paths that intertwine,
Drawing seekers to the divine.

With every twinkle, secrets rise,
Messages spun from ancient skies.
In cosmic winds, we hear a song,
A melody that pulls us along.

Nebulas bloom in radiant hues,
Painting dreams with vibrant views.
Infinite journeys, hearts ignite,
In galactic realms of endless night.

Stars are guides on this vast sea,
Whispers calling, wild and free.
Together we wander through the dark,
Chasing echoes, leaving a mark.

Whispers in the Shadows

In shadows deep, where secrets hide,
A silent world, with whispers wide.
Soft murmurs float on the evening air,
Tales of shadows, light laid bare.

The night unveils its mystic charm,
Embracing fears, yet keeping warm.
Figures dance in moon's soft glow,
Whispers echo, ebb and flow.

Paths diverge in twilight's mist,
Every heartbeat, a chance not missed.
Intrigued we wander, hearts aligned,
In whispers, fate is often blind.

Under the veil, we weave and thread,
In shadows where our dreams are fed.
Embrace the whispers, hold them tight,
For in the echoes, lives the light.

Ephemeral Glimmers

In morning's light, a soft embrace,
Whispers dance in time and space.
Fleeting moments, bright yet rare,
Traces linger, like dreams in air.

Stars that flicker, shadows cast,
Memories fade, yet hold us fast.
The fleeting hour, a gentle sigh,
Painting sunsets in the sky.

Beneath the moon's enchanting glow,
Time reveals what we can't know.
Glistening moments fade away,
Yet in our hearts, forever stay.

So cherish now, the spark of time,
In transient beauty, we find rhyme.
For life is but a fleeting spark,
Ephemeral glimmers in the dark.

Shadows of Ancient Giants

Beneath the boughs of ageless trees,
Lie stories whispered by the breeze.
Roots that cradle history's weight,
Silhouettes dark, they quietly wait.

Echoes of footsteps long since gone,
In the twilight, where dreams are drawn.
Giants watching, patient and wise,
Guardians of the earth and skies.

Their shadows stretch 'neath the evening glow,
Tales of strength only they know.
In the silence, a wisdom calls,
Within their shade, the past enthralls.

The ancient woods, a sacred space,
Where time stands still in nature's grace.
Among these giants, we stand small,
Yet find our place, connected to all.

Dreams of Hidden Realms

In the silence of twilight's embrace,
We wander through a secret place.
Veils of mist, a soft retreat,
Hidden realms beneath our feet.

Whispers echo through glades of green,
Unseen worlds where we have been.
Luminous beings, spirits unfold,
Weaving tales in threads of gold.

Through twilight paths, we dare to glide,
Into the dreams where secrets hide.
The night reveals what day conceals,
In hidden realms, all truth reveals.

So take my hand, let's drift away,
Into the night, where shadows play.
In dreams we find what's lost from sight,
In hidden realms, we meet the light.

Stories in Celestial Drift

Stars flicker in the cosmic sea,
Each a tale, a memory.
Galaxies swirl, in silence, drift,
Whispers hidden, our minds uplift.

Comets blaze through the endless night,
Trailing secrets, a fleeting light.
Constellations, maps of the past,
In their patterns, we are cast.

Voices echo from ages long,
In the heavens, they sing their song.
Every flicker, a story spun,
In celestial drift, we are one.

So gaze upon the endless sky,
Let the stars teach us to fly.
In their glow, we find our place,
Stories of time in cosmic embrace.

Murmurs of the Cosmos in Stillness

In the quiet of the night,
Stars whisper tales of light.
Galaxies spin with grace,
In the vast, serene space.

Nebulas cradle dreams,
Dancing in cosmic beams.
Time's gentle hand extends,
Where infinity blends.

Softly the silence sighs,
As comets trace the skies.
Dreamers gaze, hearts in tow,
In the ebb of the glow.

Echoes of ages past,
In the stillness, hold fast.
The universe hums low,
Murmurs only we know.

Song of the Ethereal Lyricist

Notes flutter on the breeze,
Caressing ancient trees.
Melodies weave through the air,
Songs of love everywhere.

The lyricist sings softly,
Notes spill gracefully.
Harmonies drift above,
In a dance of pure love.

Each chord a story told,
In the twilight, pure gold.
Voices blend, lost in time,
Echoes of rhythm and rhyme.

In the fabric of the night,
The song takes flight.
Ethereal sounds unite,
In the heart's pure light.

Chronicles of the Hidden Twilight

In the soft twilight glow,
Secrets linger, ebb and flow.
Shadows stretch, night descends,
Where the world quietly blends.

Pages turn in the dark,
Stories whisper, leaving a mark.
Dreams flicker like fireflies,
As the daylight softly dies.

Lost in tales of the dusk,
In the calm, a quiet husk.
Fables twine in the shade,
Where the night plans are laid.

Chronicles softly unfold,
In the silence, brave and bold.
Timeless secrets confide,
As twilight turns the tide.

Secrets Beneath the Stardust

Beneath the velvet sky,
Whispers of the stars fly.
In the dust, stories breathe,
Hiding treasures, we believe.

Each spark holds a deep tale,
Of journeys lost and frail.
Constellations align bright,
Guardians of the night.

Faint echoes of the old,
In secret tales retold.
Glimmers of past reside,
Where the mysteries hide.

Beneath celestial shroud,
The rhythms of hearts loud.
In stardust we find peace,
As the secrets never cease.

Twilight Myths

Whispers of dusk fill the air,
Secrets of shadows linger there.
Colors blend in a soft embrace,
Time stands still in this sacred space.

Legends bloom in fading light,
Tales of courage, fears of night.
As stars emerge in twilight's veil,
Mysteries weave a vibrant tale.

In the silence, dreams take flight,
Voices echo with pure delight.
Nature hums a mystic tune,
Beneath the watchful, silver moon.

Twilight curls 'round the weary soul,
Granting peace, making us whole.
The myths are born when day departs,
In the twilight, magic starts.

Ghostly Starlight

Flickering lights on a midnight shore,
Spirits dancing, longing for more.
Caught between what's real and not,
Ghostly whispers in the moonlight's spot.

Shadows move with a fleeting grace,
Veils of time, we cannot trace.
Echoes of laughter from days gone by,
Under the vast, eternal sky.

Stars align in a cosmic play,
Guiding lost souls who've gone astray.
In the silence, they gently sway,
Wishing for dawn to take them away.

Yet in this haunting, beauty lies,
Sparkling dreams in midnight skies.
Ghostly starlight, forever free,
A tapestry of memory.

Starlit Visions

Underneath the boundless night,
Dreams unfold in soft starlight.
Visions dance in cosmic streams,
Carried forth on whispered dreams.

Galaxies swirl in endless flight,
Painting visions with pure delight.
Awakening the heart's desire,
Igniting souls with celestial fire.

Through the silence, secrets bloom,
Guided by the night's sweet tune.
Wonders await in unseen realms,
Where starlit visions take the helms.

Every twinkle, a story told,
In a universe vast and bold.
The night is a canvas dark and deep,
Where starlit visions gently seep.

Enchanted Hours

Moments captured in twilight's glow,
Time stands still as dreams bestow.
In enchanted hours, hearts align,
Whispers of love in starlit f vines.

A gentle breeze caresses the night,
Carrying secrets in soft moonlight.
Colors blend in a magical dance,
Inviting souls to take a chance.

In these hours, worries fade,
A sanctuary of memories made.
Through laughter and soft, tender sighs,
Life unfolds beneath the skies.

Celebrate the magic we hold near,
Enchanted hours, forever dear.
As dusk turns to dawn and dreams take flight,
Love lingers on in the morning light.

Threads of the Void

In the darkness where whispers dwell,
Threads of silence weave and swell.
Stars unravel their ageless lore,
In the void, we seek for more.

Shadows dance on the edge of night,
Echoes flicker like fragile light.
In this tapestry, dreams intertwine,
Lost in the stillness, we redefine.

Time flows like a river wide,
Carving paths where secrets hide.
Each thread a story, each knot a fate,
In the void, we contemplate.

Beneath the cosmos, we find our place,
Threads connect in an endless space.
Woven moments, forever bound,
In the void, true peace is found.

Celestial Echoes

Whispers of stars, a gentle call,
Celestial echoes above us all.
Galaxies swirl in a cosmic dance,
In their rhythm, we take a chance.

Moonlight glimmers on silver seas,
Melodies carried by soft night breeze.
Each note a promise, resounding clear,
In the vastness, our hearts draw near.

Constellations map the skies anew,
Stories etched in a cosmic hue.
Echoes of laughter and ancient tears,
Resonate through the endless years.

In this symphony of night's embrace,
We find our rhythm, we find our grace.
Celestial echoes, forever they stay,
Guiding our souls in a timeless way.

Starfall Narratives

Falling stars weave tales untold,
Whispers of magic, dreams of old.
Beneath the sky, wishes take flight,
In the darkness, we ignite the night.

Each spark a memory, a fleeting kiss,
Stories linger in the cosmic abyss.
With every fall, a secret's shared,
In the vast universe, we are bared.

Galactic winds carry our sighs,
As constellations blink through our eyes.
Starfall narratives paint the sky,
A canvas where hopes and dreams lie.

In this moment, we rise and fall,
Together we answer the universe's call.
Starfall dreams, forever they last,
In the tapestry of time, we are cast.

Murmurs of Twilight

In the hush where daylight fades,
Murmurs of twilight serenade.
Colors blend in a gentle sigh,
Painting whispers as night draws nigh.

Crickets sing in the cooling air,
Secrets shared with a love so rare.
Shadows stretch as the stars awake,
In twilight's embrace, our hearts break.

The horizon blushes with twilight's grace,
Moments linger in this sacred space.
Between dusk and dawn, we drift and dream,
In the silence, we find our seam.

Murmurs of twilight, soft and sweet,
In this world, our souls meet.
Carried by twilight's gentle flow,
With every breath, our spirits grow.

Secrets of the Moonlit Breeze

Whispers in the dark night,
Carried by the gentle wind.
Secrets woven in moonlight,
Softly where the dreams begin.

Leaves rustle with a sigh,
Tales of lovers long since lost.
Stars above like watchful eyes,
Guarding hearts at any cost.

In shadows where mysteries hide,
Promises in silence made.
Feel the magic in the tide,
Of moments that never fade.

Underneath the silver glow,
The world slows to catch its breath.
In the night, all paths will show,
The beauty found in stillness, death.

Dreams Sown in Cosmic Dust

In the cradle of the stars,
Dreams are whispered on the breeze.
Infinity in subtle jars,
Capturing what sets hearts at ease.

Galaxies spin tales untold,
Floating softly in the vast.
Each heartbeat is a spark of gold,
Creating futures from the past.

Veils of time gently unwind,
Past and present intertwine.
In the cosmos, hope we find,
Sown in dust, by fate's design.

Awake, they dance within the night,
Guided by a timeless hand.
Illuminate with gentle light,
Embracing every grain of sand.

Echoes Beneath the Twilight Canopy

Beneath the arch of twilight dim,
Echoes linger in the air.
Silhouettes at the forest's brim,
Whispers travel everywhere.

Branches sway in soft refrain,
Nature hums a sacred song.
Each note carries joy and pain,
In the evening, we belong.

Stars awaken one by one,
Canvas painted in deep hue.
Night unveils what day has spun,
In dreams, the world feels anew.

Voices soft in shadows play,
Memories wrapped in night's embrace.
In every rustle and delay,
The twilight sings of time and space.

Silhouettes of the Sleeping Sky

Silhouettes dance on the edge,
Where daylight softly bows to night.
A tranquil world, a whispered pledge,
In the depths of fading light.

Clouds drift like thoughts unspoken,
Carried by a lullaby.
In their embrace, hearts unbroken,
Underneath the vast, deep sky.

Stars are dreams in waiting bright,
Twinkling secrets, bright and clear.
In the silence, take your flight,
Find your path devoid of fear.

As the world begins to slumber,
Beneath the canvas painted wide,
In the quiet, let hearts wonder,
Silhouettes of where dreams hide.

Phantoms in the Starlight

Whispers dance through the night air,
Ghostly figures, a fleeting stare.
They twirl beneath a silver moon,
A soft lament, a haunting tune.

Echoes of dreams long left behind,
In shadows deep, their fates aligned.
With every pulse, the stars ignite,
Phantoms move in the starlit night.

Breathe in the chill of secret sighs,
Where memories linger, forever lies.
A silent waltz on the velvet ground,
Their stories weave, lost then found.

In the hush, where whispers meet,
Fleeting glimpses, they feel so sweet.
As dawn approaches, they fade away,
Leaving echoes of shadows that stay.

Nighttime Chronicles

Under the cloak of endless skies,
A tale unfolds where darkness lies.
Stars bear witness to whispered lore,
Of lovers lost and heroes' war.

Each rustling leaf tells a story true,
The night holds secrets in shades of blue.
With every step, shadows collide,
In nighttime's embrace, we dare confide.

Moonlit paths wind through the trees,
The air is thick with memories.
A journey taken, a heart that aches,
In silence shared, a solace breaks.

Counting the stars, we mark our fate,
Time drifts slowly, we contemplate.
The chronicles weave in twilight's glow,
In nighttime's arms, we learn to know.

Flickering Flicks

Flickering lights in the evening frame,
Stories play in a soft flame.
Shadows dance on the wall's embrace,
Each moment captured, time a race.

Whispers echo from the screen's glow,
Heroes rise, and some must go.
A tapestry of dreams unfolds,
In silent cinema, the heart beholds.

A flick of fate, a twist in the plot,
In vivid hues, we find what's sought.
Laughter lingers, so does the pain,
In every flicker, a soul's refrain.

Through film we travel, near and far,
Under the light of a guiding star.
In fleeting moments, we find our home,
In flickering dreams, we freely roam.

Cosmic Cathedrals

Gaze upon the celestial dome,
In cosmic cathedrals, we find our home.
Galaxies swirl in a grand ballet,
As stardust whispers in soft array.

The universe hums a sacred tune,
Beneath the watchful eye of the moon.
Nebulae blossom, a floral surprise,
In the vast expanse, our spirits rise.

Each star a beacon of ancient light,
Illuminates the depths of night.
In echoes of time, our souls connect,
Amidst the cosmos, we find respect.

In quiet stillness, we hear the call,
Of cosmic tales that bind us all.
In cathedrals vast, our dreams take flight,
Forever bright in the endless night.

Milton Keynes UK
Ingram Content Group UK Ltd.
UKHW020735301124
451807UK00019B/787